Little Red Riding Hood Coloring Book

Karen E. Goldsmith

DOVER PUBLICATIONS, INC., *New York*

Copyright © 1992 by Karen E. Goldsmith.
All rights reserved under Pan American and International Copyright Conventions.

Published in Canada by General Publishing Company, Ltd., 30 Lesmill Road, Don Mills, Toronto, Ontario.

Published in the United Kingdom by Constable and Company, Ltd., 3 The Lanchesters, 162–164 Fulham Palace Road, London W6 9ER.

Little Red Riding Hood Coloring Book is a new work, first published by Dover Publications, Inc., in 1992.

International Standard Book Number: 0-486-27026-2

Manufactured in the United States of America
Dover Publications, Inc., 31 East 2nd Street, Mineola, N.Y. 11501

Note

Here, in coloring book form, is a delightful retelling of the classic tale of Little Red Riding Hood. You will find ready-to-color illustrations of Little Red Riding Hood and all the other characters of the story, including Little Red Riding Hood's mother and grandmother, the wolf and the hunter. Here, too, are Red Riding Hood's and her grandmother's house and the woods in between that Red Riding Hood must travel through. Have a good time coloring this exciting and timeless folktale.

Once upon a time there was a sweet little girl. Everyone loved her, but no one was more fond of her than her grandmother, who was always doing nice things for her.

4

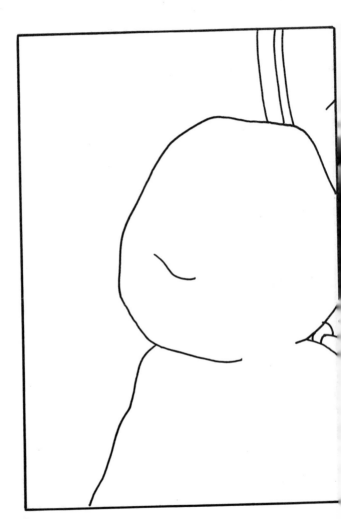

Once she made the girl a little red velvet hood that was so pretty on her that she wore it everywhere she went. And so she became known as Little Red Riding Hood.

One day her mother said to her,
"Your grandmother is very sick. I've
made some bread and butter for you

to take to her to make her feel better.
Now get started right away before the
day gets too hot. Remember: stay on
the path and don't waste time talking
to strangers. When you get there, be
polite and say good morning to her.''

Little Red Riding Hood promised her mother that she would be careful and walked to the forest where her grandmother lived. On her way through the woods she met a big wolf. She was not afraid, though, because she did not know that wolves were dangerous.

12

"Good morning, Little Red Riding Hood," said the wolf.

"Good morning, Wolf," answered the girl.

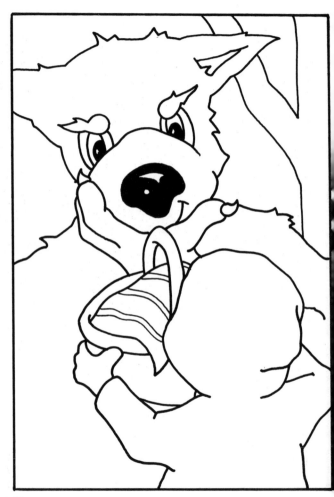

"Where are you going so early in the morning, Little Red Riding Hood?" asked the wolf.

"I am going to visit my grandmother," she answered.

"What are you carrying in your basket?" asked the wolf.

"Bread and butter my mother made. My grandmother is sick and they will help give her strength."

"Where does your grandmother live, Little Red Riding Hood?"

"Her house is a little walk from here. It stands beneath three oak trees and there are hazel bushes all around it," said Little Red Riding Hood.

18

The wolf thought to himself, "This little girl would make a delicious meal, and I would like to eat her right now. But I must figure out a way to catch her and her grandmother too."

The wolf walked alongside Little Red Riding Hood for a while and said, "Little Red Riding Hood, take time to look at the pretty flowers growing all around you and to hear the birds singing. You are just walking along as if you were on your way to school when it's so delightful here in the woods."

Little Red Riding Hood looked around her and saw the lovely sunbeams shining through the trees and the beautiful flowers everywhere. Then she had an idea. "I'll take time to pick some flowers to take to my grandmother. That will make her very happy. And since it is now early in the morning, I can still get to her house in plenty of time."

And so she ran through the forest, looking for flowers. Every time she picked one, she saw a prettier one a little farther off, and so she went farther and farther into the woods.

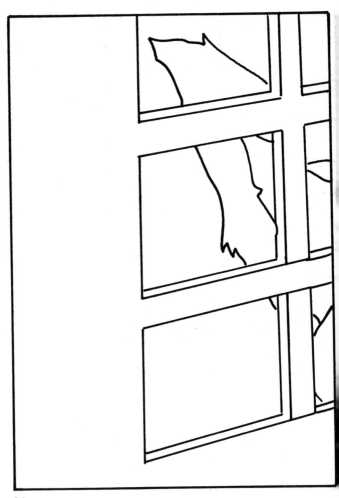

But in the meantime, the wolf went straight to the grandmother's house and knocked at the door.

"Who's there?" cried the grand-mother.

"Little Red Riding Hood," answered the wolf in a tiny voice. "I've brought you some bread and butter. Please open the door."

"Lift the latch," called the grand-mother, "I am too weak to get out of bed."

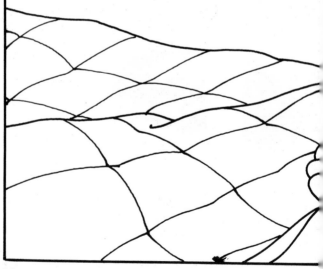

So the wolf lifted the latch, and pushed the door open.

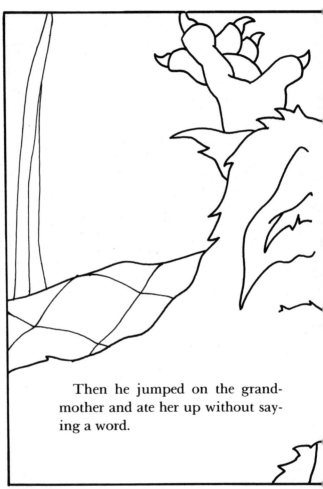

Then he jumped on the grandmother and ate her up without saying a word.

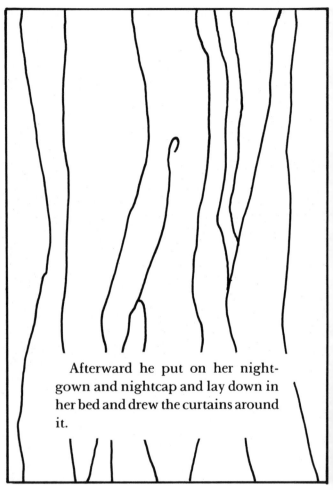

Afterward he put on her night-gown and nightcap and lay down in her bed and drew the curtains around it.

All this time Little Red Riding Hood was still running around in the woods gathering flowers. When she had picked as many as she could carry, she remembered her grandmother and started walking to her house.

She was surprised to find the door wide open and when she went inside she felt very strange and thought to herself, "Oh dear, I feel a little frightened and yet this morning I was so glad to be going to visit my grandmother!"

Little Red Riding Hood said, "Good morning, Grandmother," but there was no answer. Then she went up to the bed and drew back the curtains: she saw that her grandmother had her nightcap pulled down over her eyes so that she looked very strange.

"Oh, Grandmother!" said Little Red Riding Hood, "What big ears you have!"

"The better to hear you with," said the wolf.

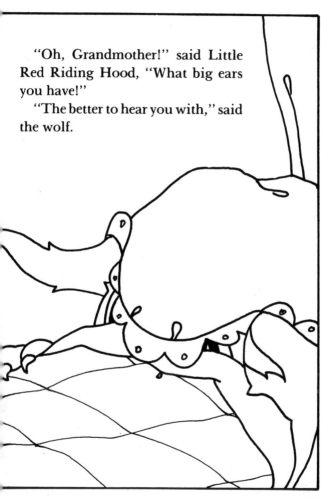

"Oh, Grandmother! What big eyes you have!" said Little Red Riding Hood.

"The better to see you with," said the wolf.

42

"And Grandmother, what big hands you have!" said Little Red Riding Hood.

"The better to hold you with," said the wolf.

"But Grandmother, what big teeth you have!" said Little Red Riding Hood.

"The better to eat you with!" And the wolf leaped from the bed in a single bound and swallowed up poor Little Red Riding Hood.

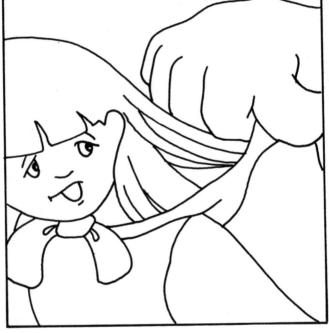

45

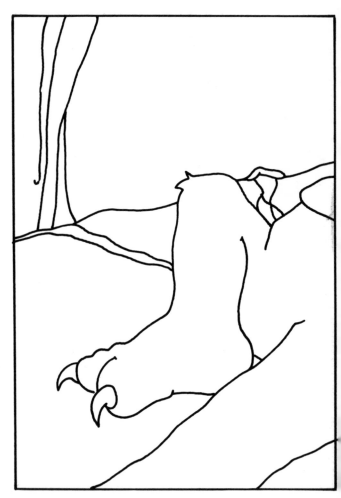

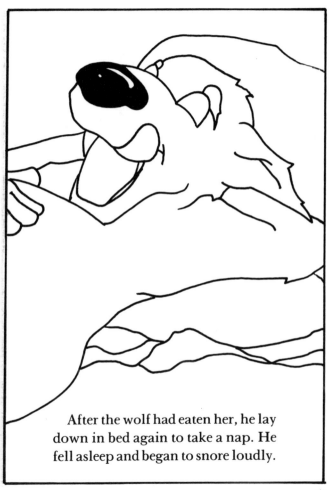

After the wolf had eaten her, he lay down in bed again to take a nap. He fell asleep and began to snore loudly.

A hunter passing the house heard
the noise and thought, "I've never
heard the old woman snore like
that—I'd better see if she's all right."

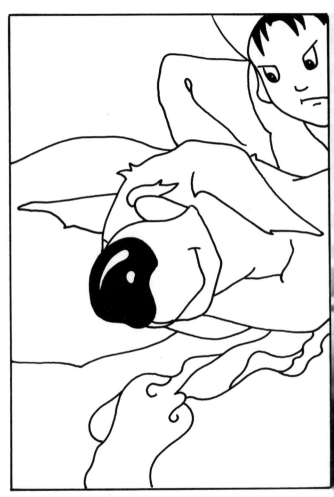

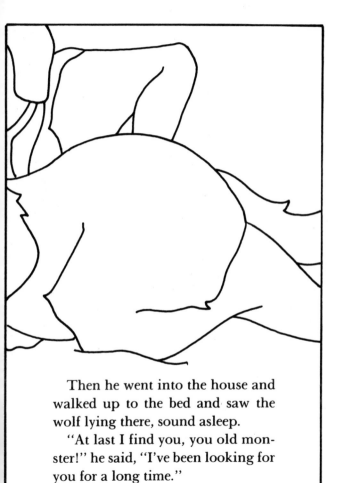

Then he went into the house and walked up to the bed and saw the wolf lying there, sound asleep.

"At last I find you, you old monster!" he said, "I've been looking for you for a long time."

The hunter thought that the wolf had swallowed the grandmother whole and that she could still be saved. So, instead of shooting the wolf, he took a pair of scissors and cut a hole in the wolf's stomach.

After a few snips, Little Red Riding Hood peeked out. After a few more she jumped out and cried, "Oh dear! I was so frightened! It's very dark inside the wolf!"

And then out came the grandmother, still alive and breathing.

Then Little Red Riding Hood went out in the yard and brought back some large stones, which she put in the wolf's stomach.

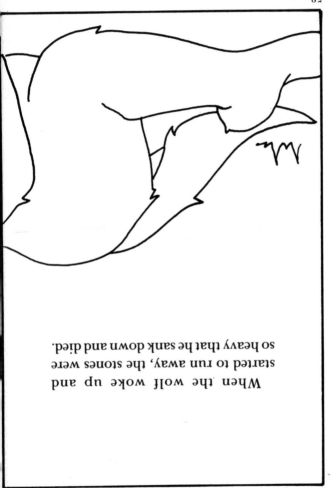

When the wolf woke up and
started to run away, the stones were
so heavy that he sank down and died.

The hunter, Little Red Riding Hood and her grandmother were filled with joy. The hunter removed the skin of the wolf and carried it home.

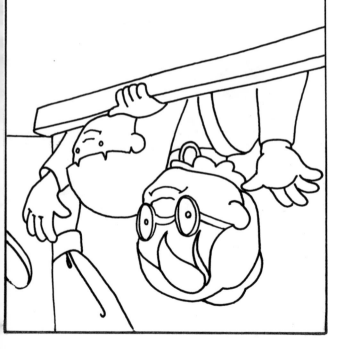

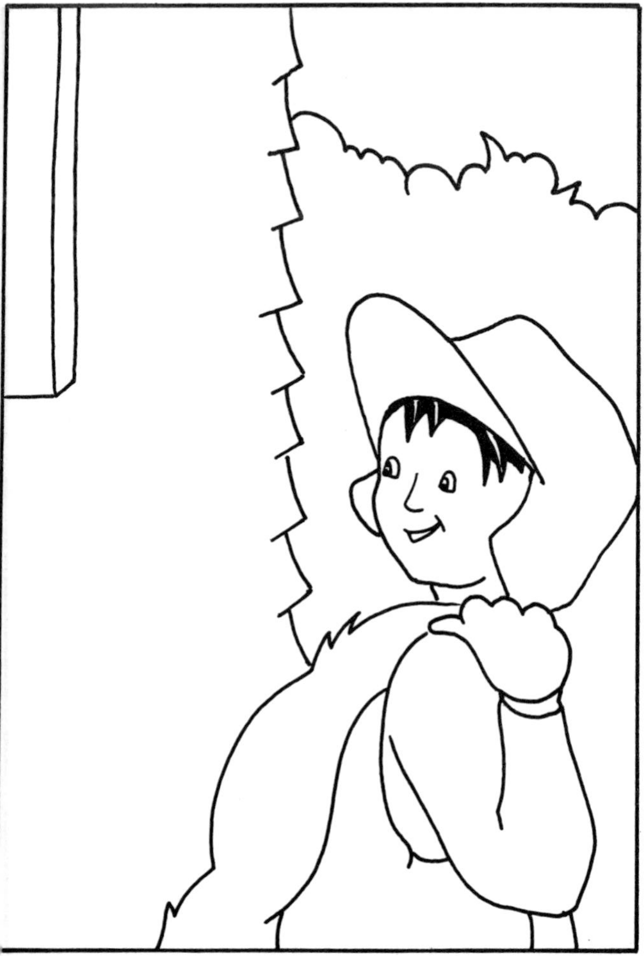

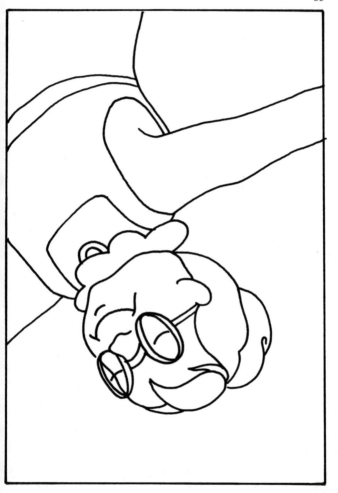

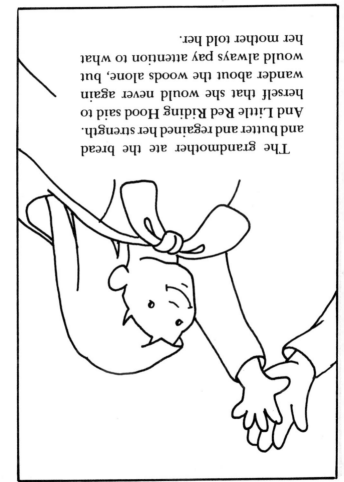

The grandmother ate the bread and butter and regained her strength. And Little Red Riding Hood said to herself that she would never again wander about the woods alone, but would always pay attention to what her mother told her.